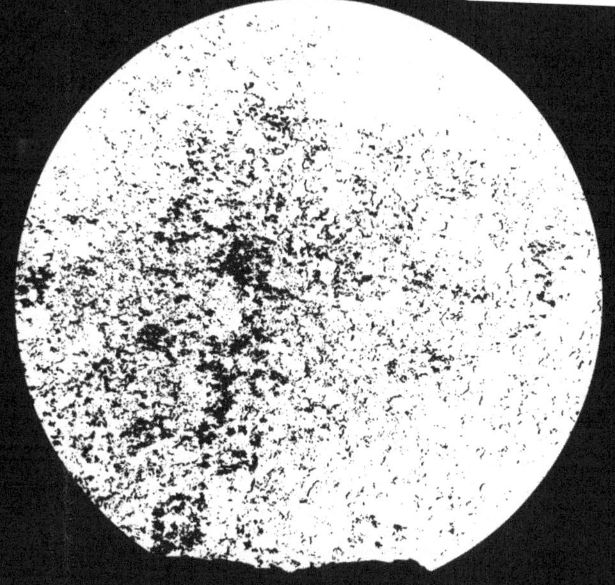

A bleeding wound, from which drips, one by one,
moments of silence...
Thoughts cut into words come back to me.
That wound trembles,
as if a heart were pumping pain into it...
I turn silent.
My body has forgotten what to do.
Words have withdrawn into me.
My breath has died.
And it's as if
some unspeakable power pulled me out of me
and carried me away.
An ugly dream...
Unfairly real!

How can a mother kill?
By failing to love!

children

[of a mother who kills]
poetry for a wounded soul

I take my thoughts and
make room for them,
in my soul.
I cover my eyes
and
let them write...
They want to tell
a story heard,
but not seen.
It's a story of
wounded souls...

The joy of birth and the feeling, for the first time,
of the warm and innocent creature filling a mother's
arms with love,
gives meaning to Divine creation.
Nothing more can fit into a mother's soul,
for there, she has everything.
All the while, misery lurks...

Although she knows the sufferings of life,
the mother soul believes, firmly,
that she will be able to protect her child.
This is her role as a MOTHER!
So happiness covers her eyes and mouth and gives her expression.
It is the expression of the triumph of a new life.

But do all mothers feel the same way?
They should.
But they don't.
Some mothers feel relief and hate.
They feel relieved to be rid of the annoying burden that
has occupied them and throw, with hatred, into the
unknown, a soul that remains nobody's.
Nobody has anything. Nobody exists.
Whose child will it be, beaten away with hatred from its
mother?

The pain of this unloved child strikes me.
I am cut by the pain of their loneliness.
I feel the bullet fired by their mother's machine gun into
their lonely little heart.
How does a mother metamorphose?
How did evil capture her, leaving her no chance at life?

With the blessing of the One who sent them,
this child will be the child of Good.
Except that sometimes Evil cheats Good
and turns it upside down.
Then Evil steals the child;
It steals that innocent and wonderful life hidden
in an uncorrupted soul.
THUS EVIL BECOMES THE CHILD'S MOTHER, AND THEN
THE ADULT IN THEM IS CONDEMNED
TO SUFFERING AND PERDITION.
Where Evil exists, there is no Love and Good,
but Hatred, Destruction, and Heartlessness.
There is only Loss.

Of self and others...

Is there pleasure in blood?
Is there pleasure in suffering?
Is there pleasure in pain?
Where do we end by madly pursuing the dark mystery of
pleasure?
It's the pleasure of a lost mind from a world of evil
that eats souls.
There it returns whenever it needs life.

Your child, you love.
Loving them makes them understand love.
Healthy souls usually love Love,
because it's tender, warm, calm, and kind.
By giving love,
your child exudes tenderness,
warmth, calm, and kindness.
Your child exudes Peace.

Deprivation of love becomes a mother's most perilous weapon.
When she withholds love for her child,
she abandons them to a destiny of self-loss.
Her child becomes a delicate feather, plucked from a wing,
carried by the wind to aimless destinations.
Unacquainted with love, the feather fails to recognize its own wing, believing it belongs elsewhere.
Unloved and abandoned, these dusty feathers amass in a cold, strange, corner, that's there only to shelter them, by chance, and not to offer them love.

Clearly, I am not made to understand the Unlove.
The Unawareness.
The Indifference.
I am not meant to be alone in a cold, empty world.
I need hearts that resonate with me and fill me with
peace.
I need to feel myself inside me and you, beside me.
I need silence when a noise disturbs my daydream.
I yearn for the refuge of dreams, when the reality I live
exposes its unsightly facets.
The ugliness that unfolds is not a mere dream;
It embodies a profound sadness and pain,
The dehumanization in its most authentic way.

Huge orange balls that end, unutterably, in heavy grey clouds...
There are massive hordes of hatred and rage exploding pointlessly...
There are hordes of frustration and injustice that drown in dust...
People and lives are dying.
Other minds have decided so.

What causes certain minds to become blind and forfeit their humanity?

Humanity, in its wholeness, is made of body and soul.
The body is the Mind.
The soul is the Love.
A human being is not complete without their Love.
They are like an unwritten book that they try to load with scribbles.
The scribblings are not stories, not even memories.
The scribbles are anxiety and turbulence.
It's the first phase of the war that a human being wages... within.

I'm not trying to answer the world,
but to find my own answers,
to accept that I still live in a world of God
and I haven't gone to hell.
Why does Earth increasingly resemble what we humans
imagine Hell to be?
Why don't we humans, in our unnatural curiosity, first
want to know Heaven?
Perhaps because, in His boundless love, God has filled
us with happiness
and we humans, in our unbounded loss of mind, want to
show Him that God is us...

Why don't bad people like us, good people?
Why doesn't their heart resonate with ours?
What is it about us that is so different, making them lose
their minds and hurt us?
What do bad people know that we, as good people,
don't?
Do bad people know that they are not eternal?
Do they realize that, like us good people, they are made
of flesh and blood?
Are they aware that, like us good people, they live on the
same earth?
Do they recognize that, like us good people, when they
are hungry, they eat, and when they are thirsty, they
drink?
Do bad people know that, like us good people, they
breathe the same air?
Our mechanisms of functioning are so similar, yet the
differences are huge.
Somewhere in this intricate mechanism, something has
lost its way...

Is insanity a form of wickedness or losing a game with yourself?
It sounds like insanity, in the true form of a foolish mind, exceeds malice.
Insanity goes beyond the being's ability to relate to life anymore.
It is the prerogative of a mind that no longer understands anything but itself.

How, indeed, are we to be spared mad minds?
Not the beautifully mad, love-sick ones,
but those gravely sick with hatred and contempt.
Minds sick with a disdain for life
and a love for evil, suffering, and despair.
Minds that do not understand.
They don't grasp that we are all creations of the same
great loving force,
and by not loving one another,
we break the magic.
Beyond this magic, we become nothing.
We lose ourselves.
We disappear.
One by one.

And disappearing one by one, nothing will be ours.
We'll have nothing left to fight for.
And then, what was the point of our lives?
Of our being on earth?
DEATH?
We are born to live, and our departure must be a
beautiful ending to a thick novel.
We are not born to kill each other,
for then what is the point of LIFE?

How do we help the sick minds that kill us?
We don't stand a chance.
There are more and more, and it's getting worse.
You look around, and you see hate.
You see need, desperation, and screaming.
You see bombs, you hear sirens.
You see scared people, orphaned children.
You see death.
Whose life must this be?

I do not glorify death!
I couldn't possibly, as long as I love my life so much.
I love my parents and my children.
I love my family.
I love people just like me.
I'm not looking in history;
I'm looking in my soul.
In the mind, never.
For my mind is dominated by my soul.

How can I support a war?
Why should I?
Why would I support people dying?
People just like me.
Children like mine.
Families just like mine, to be destroyed for no reason, no
stake.
I die, you die.
You don't hold the secret to immortality,
do you understand?
Why do you feel the need to harm?
Why do you feed on it?
What do you take with you when you die?
Land, wealth, money, bank accounts?
What do you take with you, lost soul?
You take your sins, to multiply in that world you'll end up
in, where you'll melt away for all your sick and hateful
pleasures.
Would you, who would have war, want to feel war?
To feel the pain?
How would it be to feel a big claw and some snarling
fangs tearing at you for pleasure?
That's not war; that's suffering.
Even if war is just an abstract notion, its expression is
the most hateful, and it's called SUFFERING...
... Suffering taken to extremes by lost minds that
innocent people feel.

You, evil, you're destructive!
Me, I don't understand your stake.
It's beyond me.
Maybe because I don't want to know you, I can't
understand you.
But you know what, evil?
Could you make a world of your own and leave mine?
Could you leave my world clean and green?
That's the way my world used to be...

I don't want to fall prey to evil minds.
I hide from them.
I retreat into myself or my home, hoping they won't invade.
I want to live.
But not to live to seek answers to pointless questions.
I want to live to find answers to the questions of my soul.
I want to discover the earth with its beauties.
I want to know people, with their beauty.
I want to offer the world the goodness and beauty of my soul.
My soul does not understand wickedness, but it understands that this wickedness is not barren.
And that worries it.

Why are rich people not necessarily happy people?
Why does money not guarantee happiness?
Why don't big houses and expensive cars guarantee happiness?
Why don't jewels and fancy clothes bring sparkle to the eyes?
After all, where does our happiness lie?

The happiness of each of us is right there,
where we feel it.
And if we don't feel it there, it's not there.
No material thing brings it to us.
Then, what are we fighting for?
Does mankind fight wars to regain goodness?
Does mankind fight wars to regain generosity?
Does mankind fight wars to regain sincerity?
Does mankind fight wars to regain peace?
Why are wars never for the soul?
Why do we care so little for our souls and glorify our
bodies so much when the soul is everything?
A sad man weeps.
An unhappy man makes others unhappy too, because
that's the only way they can bear their suffering.

Wickedness is not new.
It's not something that sprang up overnight.
Neither are wars.
People have been fighting wars for as long as they can remember.
We've always lived in communion with evil, and maybe, because if we didn't have it with us, we wouldn't realize how good Good is.
However, for a while now, Evil seems to be trying to take us over.
We don't care about ourselves anymore.
About our children.
About the legacy they will inherit on this Earth.

We have no respect for life.
We have no respect for ourselves.
We love our car, we love our new coat, or maybe our
latest gadget.
That's where our care goes.
We love relationships of completeness and often ignore
honesty.
Words will always be too small for the soul.
Maybe that's why we don't even bother
to use them wisely.

What chance has life in the face of death where there is
war?
What chance has a small heart to become a big heart
where there is war?
The chances of that small heart are breathing hard.
They seem to carry a burden.

But for some, that doesn't matter.

I won't forget the moments I had two summers ago in
my village in the highlands.
How beautiful it was!
And quiet! It's quiet in my village.
There are geese, cows, horses, pigs, ducks, chickens,
and sheep.
In my village, there's green grass and chirping birds.
There are streams where animals drink.
In my village, trees bloom in spring and bear fruit in
autumn, just like the earth.
It smells of flowers and animal dung.
It also smells of smoke from burning leaves and wood
burned in the stove in winter.
It smelled of war a long time ago,
in my great-grandparents' time...

I don't necessarily want to know, but...
what does war smell like?
It smells like pain.
I think it smells most like pain.
And suffering.
And despair.
And screaming.
And crying.
And fear.
And horror.

War must smell of blood and bodies...

I do not judge war or the decisions of minds.
My mind, guided by my soul, judges situations and facts.
I think I am fragile and vulnerable.
Extremely vulnerable, squeezing the needs of all the
victimized souls into me.
Maybe war is for strong people, not for the likes of me.
My dog died recently.
Then, in my soul, I felt pain.
My mother died too, long ago.
Then, I felt liberation.
Why?
Because my mother no longer had to endure the
colossal pain that plagued her frail body...
I love you, Mom, beyond everything!

Why are wars angry, wrathful, and cold?
Why can't humans rise above the malice that dominates
them?
I think the souls of humans are like mine.
Weak and vulnerable.
It's called sensitivity.
Our souls are sensitive.
Or is our soul also called sensitivity?
It seems that sensitivity embodies everything: love,
kindness, goodness, passion, warmth, caring, concern,
compassion, peace...
No trace of war!
What does war feel like?

Where is its place in our being?!...

I close my eyes and let the bullet of lost time pass me by.
I realize it didn't touch me, and I start over.
I want to regain my strength to succeed.
It's a war between me and me;
between me and my victorious forces.
It's me, myself, and the universe.
Once again.

If I had a superpower, I would gather all the children in the world and read them stories.
If I had a superpower, I would embrace all the children of the world in a warm and loving hug, letting them experience eternal happiness.
If I had a superpower, I would want all the children of the world to never see the Ugly and never know the Evil that surrounds them.
If I had a superpower, I would invite all the children of the world to color the world in the most beautiful colors.

IF I HAD A SUPER SUPERPOWER, I WOULD MAKE ALL THE CHILDREN OF THE WORLD IMMORTAL.

And if they had a superpower, I'm sure all the children of the world would proclaim
FOREVER peace.

I look long and wonder
if the sea is beautiful for its endless blue or
if its blue contrasts so much with the sandy ruins that
border it, as to enhance its infinity.
On the sea, there is peace.
In the sand, there is war.
Between them, a common border, washed by the sea,
devoured by sand.

I see how, timid and trembling,
from behind a ruin,
a dusty little face shyly approaches,
looking for their mother.
I take their hand and kiss it.
In that shy, sad hand,
they will feel love no more...

In a wheelchair, a dry, pale old woman wears her story on
her face.
War seems to have drawn the sap that once clothed her
body,
leaving behind a sad shadow.
A life near its end still begs for salvation...

A stooped old man shuffled his steps, trying to drag the
whole past behind him.
Although he had nothing left behind, his steps seemed
heavy.
His old hand sheltered all his wealth:
his holy family in a sliver of time...

Children don't care what country they live in.
Children live happily with their mother and father
Children live happily with their brothers and sisters.
Children find peace in their safe and loving family.
When their safe and loving family is broken
and brothers and sisters are lost,
when mom and dad suddenly head off into the unknown,
children are left alone.
Then children know loneliness.
And they live in fear.
The war has broken all their soul ties
The WAR...
... a word so NOT for children!...
Children don't have anger, hatred, pride.
Children have innocence and goodness.
Why does war hate innocence and goodness?

A doll's head stared blankly out from under a pillow covered in ruins.
There, once, had been life.
The war had wiped life from this home and left it to perish.
With it once, many blank, still, cold stares...
Who had banished life from this home?

I walk among the nameless ruins,
Everything weeps and burns.
The rages of war swallow up life, anonymously.
What once was life is left without face and identity.

I lift my eyes to heaven to beg for mercy.
Mercy for all the children of the world whom war has
made evil.
I lift my eyes to heaven and beg for goodness.
Goodness for all the children of the world whom war has
made evil.
I lift up my eyes to heaven and beg for PEACE.
Grant that the children of the world may live!

I don't know what strength it takes to watch
one man-made thing undo another God-made thing.
It seems to me too much that mankind is at odds with
God.
And to see how small and insignificant we are,
God leaves us alone.
We, alone, don't know how to save ourselves.
We, alone, are sinking.
We sink in ignorance and pride,
In anger, hatred, and revenge.
We sink in the mire of evil because that's all we can do.
Lord, give our walk a meaning!

Mothers with babies in their arms seek healing
for war-torn souls...
Children cry and need nurturing cuddles.
Fathers search for places to hide their helplessness.
Wars transfigure people and realities...

WHERE IS GOD?

God turns his back on the wickedness of people.
God is not part of hatred.
The world, God's creation, is possessed by Evil.
And God leaves it to its own destruction.
Help one another, people!
God will always be there to help you if you ask for his help,
because God is in every one of us.

Out of the turmoil of a troubled heart,
I describe a piece of peace...
A boat cuts through the sea that washes its deck.
It seems to be drifting, when, in fact, the boat is living its
moment of peace in full communion with the Sea...

It's not much to go up, but it's so little to go down...
Virtues have hidden themselves from us and transformed themselves into huge, insurmountable mountains.
They have left us prey to the abysses that suddenly swallow us up when we lose hold of our virtues.
We are easy prey to the other side of ourselves...

By hand, all the children of the world draw peace.
It's blue with yellow and green.
It's water, sun, and the earth all together.
Inside there is peace.
Beyond them... dying rage!
It's the realm of perverted humans.
It's the land of pain and suffering.
Of make-believe and convention.
It is the land of dishonest puppets, unfairly and unjustly handled.
Dolls have no mind or life of their own.
They are pulled by strings to be as some pathetic actors want them to be.
They are us, with us, for us.
We lie to each other.
We're miserable.
We sink and we seem to be so far from our childhoods.

Why is the music of war so grave and sinister?
Because it is music that announces death.
With accents of tubas and violins.
It sounds shrill and frightening.
War music brings death from the first note.
My blood is sickened.
My ears do not accept it.
Go and unmake the ears of those who play you,
Music of death!

I'm hitchhiking so someone can pick me up and hide me
in the sun.
I need peace and understanding.
I need kindness and peacefulness.
There, in my world, all the lonely children are waiting for
me.
We pray together so that we stay.
And love each other.
And color the world again and give it light.
And then send the wind to clean the traces of war.
Then we drip from the stars a magic dust to restore the
glow of hope for Good.
We hold hands and beg the sky to rain down and bring
life to the desolate world.
Beneath us, the stones that hide dead life...

War is the hiding of death-hungry brains.
...what's the point of war?!
Anger and violence are not pleasing to humans.
No man can live in hiding from anger and violence.
Anger, violence, and killing are not attributes of humanity.

A corner of a photograph torn by a raging fire has an eye.
It looks like a girl's eye.
Cheerful, clear, smiling.
It's a testimony to a stillness soaked into the paper.

A little further on, under a big pile of irons,
a teddy bear's paw seems to want to scrape.
The bombs have torn it apart,
and the walls have turned his face grey.
The teddy bear is dead, but the teddy bear tried.
His paw is there for freedom.

What a striking contrast!
The sky clear blue, the sun clear yellow
The air, clear grey
The dark red blood beneath the dark grey ruins.
Pain, deep black.
The colors of war are revered by huge fireworks that
devour everything when they meet life.

Two children share a lollipop.
How do they share it?
They take turns licking it.
Two brothers,
boys with curly hair, thin lips, and lost looks,
try to soak up the sweetness of their lollipop
and pass it on to their mother's gentle, tender face,
where there is stillness and unhappiness.

Why are we so mean to sacrifice our children?
What are we made of?
Who made us this way?
What made us this way?
Why don't we take care of our children?
Why don't we, all, love children?

The raindrops that swirl on a little girl's face
are tragically mingled with the tears
that flood her eyes and the pain that gnaws at her being.
With hands to her ears,
in an attempt at forced movement,
she drags a yellow plastic truck behind her.
In it, her entire borrowed family:
a doll, a rabbit, and two pieces of broken pencils!

I hate wars!
Yes, I hate them with all my being.
I hate destructive and unthankful death,
I hate the contempt of dark minds
for all that makes me human.
What's the use of so many wars?
Why don't we care about people
and care so much about our hatred and malice
that we give them so much power?

Sing to heaven about life,
that it may glorify it!
Sing to the trees about life,
so that they may cherish it!
Sing to the sun about life,
to keep it from growing cold!
Sing to the sea about life,
So that it may stir it with joy!
Sing to the soul about life,
so that it knows it's his!

It's impossible for me to enter,
even in thought, the mind of a man who does not respect
life,
who does not love life,
who mocks God.
A man without faith remains only a body without a head.
There is nothing there to guide him,
and, as a result, he drifts down the path of ultimate
wickedness,
which devours him with lust.

I wonder what the war criminal's faith is.
What does the war criminal believe in?
Why are we afraid to judge?
Why are we afraid to say what hurts us?
We live accepting war because maybe it's not ours.
But we dread the prospect.
If, one day, that troubled mind, without God,
takes its war and brings it to our door?
Then what will our eyes see?

It seems to me that we have reached a life where we no
longer belong.
We are no longer our own.
We belong to those who think they own us.
We have become so many and so insignificant.
We are like dust on the road.
No one stops to admire the dust particles anymore.
They trample it underfoot.

I was born to live.
I was born alone.
I'm going to die that way.
No one was with me when I was born.
There will be no one with me when I die.
I came alone, I'll go alone.
But in the meantime, let me live!
With all my people by my side...

Diseases take people. Rich and poor.
Money and power are nothing.
Suffering is pain and it's the same for the powerful and the humble.
It's no use trying to satisfy a personal pride,
when there's someone out there, above you, who can prove you wrong every moment.
Has anyone ever managed to tell the dead to go away and let him live because he's rich?
Or has anyone ever managed to tell the dead to go away and let him live because he's powerful?
Or has anyone ever managed to tell the dead to go away and let him live because he has a certain social standing?
These are illusions born of unread minds...

I pass a kindergarten on my street.
A large crowd of cheerful voices covers my eyes.
Beyond the open window is life living.
Beyond the open window is hope.
Beyond the open window is love.
And Joy.
And there's something else, beyond the big noise.
There's carelessness.
There's peace!

What if the silence of my night
was violently broken by a deafening noise?
What if the sky of my world were lit by unnatural fireworks?
What would my life be?
What would my life mean?
What about my children?
What about my family?
We would suddenly become all of us,
no one's.
No one's and theirs only!
It would be that moment when people became objects.
Useless objects you can do without...

We are so different, that the inability of our minds gives me the creeps.
It doesn't matter much that I am educated, that I have studied, that I think civilized and can help the world in many ways.
In front of it, I lose my identity and meaning.
I don't matter anymore...

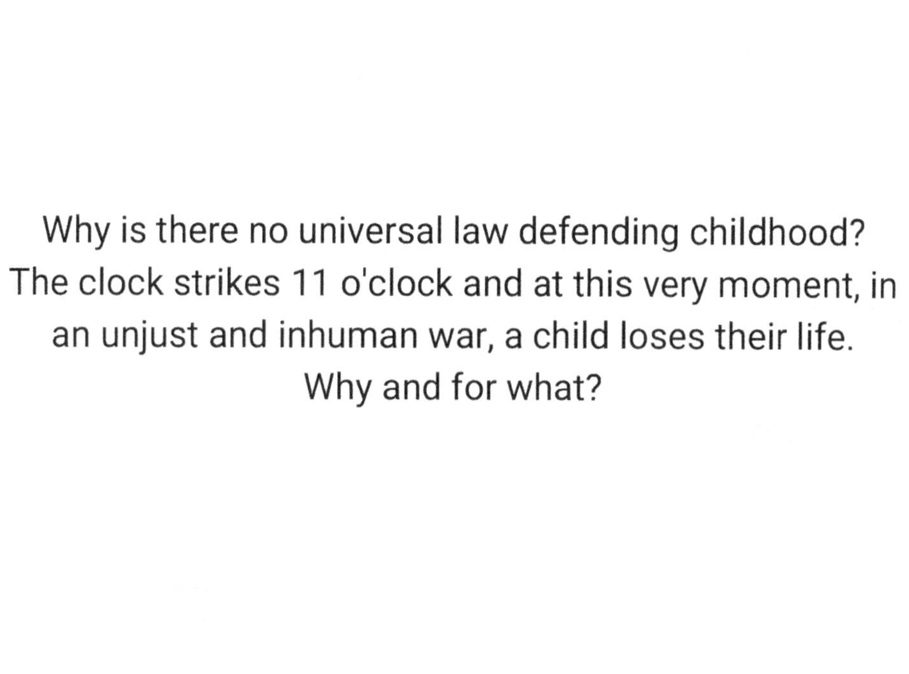
Why is there no universal law defending childhood?
The clock strikes 11 o'clock and at this very moment, in
an unjust and inhuman war, a child loses their life.
Why and for what?

Perhaps war belongs to the grown-ups,
to those who believe in it and want to fight.
But the children?!...
It pains me to hear that there are children trained
to fight from a young age.
It's not their choice, of course.
Why aren't those children trained from a young age to
LOVE?

The right to life is an unwritten law that we should all respect with sanctity.

I would give the world peace to cherish and raise it.
To the sky, I would give the birds and the sun.
To the earth, the trees, and the flowers.
To the seas, mysterious depths.
To the forest, mysterious darkness,
and to life, the people.
To all these, I would give peace.
To cherish it!

My words lose their meaning when surrounded by
passion.
They seem to search for their meaning and don't know
how to put themselves in order.
My feelings are rushing and seem to want to burst.
My mind tempers them and puts everything in order.
Together we manage to control the helplessness,
making each other better, learning respect.

I thank my God for Peace,
For my Children and my Family.
I thank my God for All I have,
For my upbringing, for my love, for my home.

I thank my God for listening to me,
and always making me understand my meaning.
Thank you, God, for keeping me human!

Perhaps your God is called differently,
Praise the One you believe in!
Faith is precisely that super force that helps us evolve
and cherish.
When we don't value what our God gives us, our God
takes it away.
Maybe not in the moment, but in time...

Let us treasure our God and his perfect work.
Thus, we humans, with faith in our God, will gain eternal
life.

I would like to banish war and take it away from the
world on the wings of the evil that carries it.
Curse it to self-destruct with its wickedness and
ugliness.
I'd like to tell War that my world doesn't want it.
That my world doesn't need it.
But War tells me he has allies who believe in it.
Then, War, go to your allies and crush them!
Let the rest of us fall prey to Love and Good,
and we'll try to make do...

I rise from the arms of my broken chair,
letting it creak to immortality...
I'm going to get some books to fill my thoughts again
And glorify me with words.
When the seeing hurts, the words soothe...

PEACE!